MEANING OF LIFE

TO BECOME ALL YOU CAN BECOME

Lois B. Mayette

Author's Tranquility Press
ATLANTA, GEORGIA

Lois B. Mayette/Author's Tranquility Press
3900 N Commerce Dr. Suite 300 #1255
Atlanta, GA 30344, USA
www.authorstranquilitypress.com

Ordering Information:
Quantity sales. Special discounts are available on quantity purchases by corporations, associations, and others. For details, contact the "Special Sales Department" at the address above.

Meaning Of Life: To Become All You Can Become / Lois B. Mayette
Paperback: 978-1-965075-92-0
eBook: 978-1-965075-93-7

PREFACE

It is said that everyone has a good book in them. The good book is one of their experiences. This is my book of experiences. It is meant to help you navigate more easily through your life as a process. Failing to see life as a process leaves much of life not making sense. You're born, you live, and you die. What is life all about?

My field of study and learning has been human behavior, so naturally I will come from my training and studies. What I experienced is not new and has been written about many times, but my perspective is from my experience in human behavior. It is for you to test and try to see if it will help you, but try not to see it as the only way to the meaning of life. Like everything in life, there are many ways to achieve meaning, and that can be the beauty. It is not about others agreeing with your or my way; growing is about having different options. The more options you have, the more choices and the more possibilities for who or what you can become.

Change is constant, so fearing change is not necessary. If it is not necessary, then working on the fear of change is a prerequisite to growth.

Our culture is at an all-time high in fears, as well as adolescence at its best. Getting help from outside yourself, like our culture, is not going to move you beyond adolescence. You will need to go inside yourself, to what is already there in your potential to grow. You likely have been in the habit of going outside yourself, to the so-called experts in the areas you seek change. That will not help you advance beyond culture. Il-me direction is now to go inside, finding your potential. Others cannot discover the unique you.

Of essence is the using of a holistic approach of body, mind, and spirit. There is a need of balancing all three areas of being. body needs exercise, healthy diet, and grooming. The mind needs inspiration, stimulation, and challenges. The spirit, the essence of you, needs growth and development.

DEFINITIONS ESSENTIAL TO THE UNDERSTANDING OF THESE CONTENTS

Awareness: cognizant of; the knowing of.

Cognition: thinking; the process of knowing.

Culturally: the United States's development; as in the mind of the US.

Detachment: to be disconnected or separate from the main body; transcending; letting go of ego so growth can take place.

Ego: the known self; the conscious self. "The self," is the potential self.

Elusive energy: hard to understand, not visual, baffling.

Ignorance: not yet known; unknown.

Imagination: power of the mind to form mental concepts.

Intelligence: the power to understand.

Introspection: the going into your own mind.

Intuition: the power of knowing things without conscious reasoning.

Meaning of life:	becoming your potential.
Metaphysical:	the mind of the universe; unknowns or not yet known.
Miracles:	an abnormal event that cannot be explained by known natural laws.
Own will:	owning your choices and responsibilities.
Paradigm shift:	major shift, taking your old model and reconstructing it to fit a new model.
Process:	a series of acts or thinking that changes the past outcome or belief.
Religion:	rituals, laws and observances, difference for each faith.
Senses:	beyond, feeling, touching, smelling, sight and hearing to intuition or still small voice.
Spirit:	the essence of you, your energy, soul, the universal mind (not religion).
Spontaneous:	unforced, natural, voluntary.
Meaning of Life:	to become all you can become.

Mankind is able to obtain truth by intensive search into the deepest recesses of all categories of natural and supernatural (which may be natural but we just don't understand them as such) phenomena. Thisbook in not about wanting or needing to prove anything scientifically, because it's not the only path to knowledge or understanding. There are more than five senses, and the ones not recognize or used more frequently are the most exciting, as we cannot cause them. They have to be experienced; that is key, experienced. Try as you may, you likely will not be able to produce the experiences. Many have tried through drugs and other experiments. (i.e., O'Leary).

"Spontaneous" can be defined as naturalness, unforced, voluntary or done of one's own will. Now, before you take this to mean I have control of the situation, "own will" here means coming from within. I can't will something to happen just because I want it to. It can happen if I have processed my will to the degree that I am ready for it to happen, knowingly or not. I may be aware of being ready for this step, or I may have the experience which will tell me I was ready.

Near-death experiences and out-of-body experiences are prime examples of experiences not produced. Enough has been said in trying to prove them one way or the other. The purpose here is to help you understand the process of your life. That. is the purpose of this book: to help do the processing of your life.

My out-of-body experience, some 30 years ago, was spontaneous. I, at the time, had no knowledge of such an experience. Later, on one occasion, my life passed before me. On neither occasion was I stressed or in any life-threatening situation. Neither did I ask for or know how to produce the experience. I. was awake during both experiences. I was not depersonalizing, no thoughts about death nor real fears of death or dying. In fact, the experience was just reassuring and positive. Looking back now, there was a conscious and subconscious desire for the "meaning of life." That's where it sent me and where I have been for the past thirty-plus years: on the quest for the "meaning of life." It is my hope that I might help you in your journey in processing your life. "Ask and you shall receive" and "No pain, no gain" come to mind now, as it's a lot of hard work, but well worth it. It, of course, will be different for everyone, but if you don't know it is a process, you will just live life without seeing how it all fits together for you. You know where you have been (maybe), where you want to go (maybe), and now you need to know how to get there from here.

OUT OF YOUR MIND

The first step is to be out of your mind—not as insane, but as putting your old beliefs aside so new ideas can come together for you and for the higher learning to take place. In order to evolve with new thinking, you must be willing first to understand you know very little. lien you need to be willing to let go of your old ideas, add to them, or expound on them. Very likely, that which you knew yesterday was not wrong or right; it was just where you were. Now, to move forward, you have to le: go of that or be willing to see it from a different perspective. It then can take on a new dimension, a very important new dimension. It can be called higher learning or thinking, insight, awareness, or enlightenment.

The mind is a powerful tool. Tie mind is nct just in the brain. There is evidence that each cell in your body has a mind. The mind is energy, more than anything else. It is not tangible, but there is evidence that it survives after death. This is important, as the choices you focus on during your life here should be a concern of yours. This leaves you responsible for choices to what you want to put in your mind to survive you after your death.

The first act that likely happens after death is you will review your life. Ask yourself if what you have been watching, reading, and focusing on will advance your growth and development. Television, movies, news, and books are important to consider in this advancing of the human race. Here is the issue tc ponder: have sex crimes decreased in the US? Has the use of drugs and alcohol decreased in the US? Has violence decreased in the US? Have depression and fears or anxiety decreased in the US? The answer to all these is no, our culture is not in a better place. Everything you put in your mind does not have to be productive, but if most of what you do is mindless, then what will you process in the first act after death? A challenging, active mind may save your mind. Alzheimer's may be warded off by a stimulating mind.

Reading is very important, but what you read is important. If you read romance novels, ask yourself if this reading has increased your romantic ability or just made you feel never satisfied or helped you stay stuck in a dream world. Remember, one out of five in our culture could be classified as depressed. The romantic novels are more likely to make you feel you're not getting the love you deserve. Now, here is the kicker. It is not about what you get from others—it is about the love you show yourself. In our culture, we live through others quite often. Look at our interest and fascination with actors and actresses. We idealize them even though their lives are, for the most part, disastrous. Before you say I am too critical, think of the drugs, alcohol, anorexia, sex, and failure to establish healthy relationships that go on in that lifestyle. Stress is primary for actors and actresses, as it is such a questionable career with so many factors not in their control.

Life is baffling until one becomes wise. In the "Peter Principle," a person rises to the level of their incompetence. It is a wise and well-adjusted person who knows where that is in self and decides not to rise there. To become wise, one must have a high sense of self. though painful at times, finding oneself is exciting, as it is the ultimate of discoveries. The answer to why man is the highest being on earth is because he has the ability to think, feel, and reason as well as respond beyond the other animals. Wisdom is not complicated; maybe that is why most don't have it. It is rather simple. It is like common sense, if not common sense. In this day and age, most are looking to brilliance for the answers. It cannot be found there, because brilliance complicates.

The other day, a theologian said he was baffled by God's commandment to make no images of God.

It's very simple: how can you make an image of God, for God is spirit? So all images would be wrong, and how can you believe in something that is wrong? We are all made in his image, so that cannot be physical; it must be spiritual. We are spiritual beings having a human experience. We are all different. If you want to be baffed over our differences even so we may have the same parents. We are different of spirit as well as physical. When things do not ring true, they likely are not true. Every time I heard a scientist make a statement as if it were gospel, I would laugh, because they usually were complicating that which is simple. They are trying to prove that something was there to begin with, and that is why it is that way. Nice try, but maybe it is there because it got utilized that way. Females are less likely to be good mathematicians than males. Scientists have been alluding to this for years. The differences in the brain was the reasoning given. I contend that it is learned. What were females told? "Math is hard and better left for males." Well, in high school, I majored in math (I'm no youngster), and all my math teachers were females. It came very natural for me. Each year, I would tell my math teacher that I did not want to take math the next year because I did not think that I would be using math when I got out of school, and she would have this little speech about math being the training for thinking. I am indebted to her today, as I am a thinker. You can see how I must have been at hearing that girls were not good in math. I was likely one of those contradictions that made me quest for the truth. Can you not see how important it is to believe in yourself here? It was apparent to me at a young age, that if it did not ring true, it likely was not. That's when the need to trust oneself and have a sense of self was important.

Self-esteem needs to be defined by breaking down the two words. First, the self, than secondly, esteem. The self, meaning the individual you. It is not focusing on others; it is focusing on the self. Esteem is the total you. Esteem refers to the level or essence of being. You are that you are—your respect of yourself. You have potential. What is your potential? You can now see that the focus is on you. It is not to others you need to look. It is in you. This should really excite you. Self-examination is essential, though a life time journey. Intelligence may be a part of your talents, but not all of you. What else are you? They say that the jails are full of high IQ's. So intelligence isn't enough; you need to be able to utilize it for your advantage, namely find out who you are and build your self-esteem. Everyone is intelligent—that is, they have the power to reason. So say, "I am intelligent," and begin there.

IGNORANCE IS CONSTRICTED AWARENESS

Ignorance is defined as the state of being without knowledge. It has little to do with intelligence. It can be said that you are ignorant about anything or parts of anything you have not as yet the knowledge of. I am ignorant about many topics and choose to be. They are topics I find of no value to me or have no interest in at the present time. (Present time as I am always changing). At the time of September 11, 2001, I realized I knew next to nothing about the Muslim religion. I was ignorant. Not only of the Muslim religion, but the Hindu, which is the oldest of religions; Buddhism, which is really a way of life rather than a religion; but Judaism and Christianity I knew the most. I was somewhat embarrassed about my lack of knowledge of other religions, so I embarked on growing and learning. Four years later, I know very little, but a lot more than I did. I realized that I could not be a good Christian (follower of Christ) if I did not know why I would choose to be, or am, a Christian. It was a wonderful adventure, and I fell in love with them all, for I discovered that at the basic level, we all believe the same. They truly are my brothers and sisters.

Buddhism states that man's mind is the creative center of his/her universe and that this mind has infinite capacity for change and growth. Having said that, it helps to see where the process center is. It is in your thinking. You are what you think! You are what you believe! Now, if what you think or believe are no longer working for you, you need to seek understanding which will add a dimension, or a twist, even, to your knowledge. The mind is a powerful tool, so thinking is what can change how to see yourself as well as the world around you. Cognition is the word used for thinking. Cognitive dissonance is a state in which intellectual comprehension completely conflicts with direct experiences. This you will struggle with frequently in your struggle to be you. Linear thinking is that which can only be seen, and mistrust especially of the self, and anything other than rationalism is a product of fear and ignorance, the lack of knowledge.

Confucius said, "Those who are meant to hear will understand, and those who are not meant to understand will not hear.

We need to acknowledge that we need help to understand. A willingness is especially a necessity. We always seem to seek outside ourselves for the answers, but the answers are more likely to be inside us already. "Greater is it that is in you than that which is in the world." Culture in the United States tries to get you to look outside, to them, but it is not there. You were born with potential, and it's up to you to pull that potential out of yourself.

"Man's main task in life is to give birth to himself." Quoted from Erich Fromm.

Who are the ones that want us to follow rather than lead? The United States is adolescence at its best. So if you follow the lead of our government, the likelihood of your becoming a healthy adult is slim. You can get help up to the phase of adolescence. After that, you are on your own. "Come as a little child" isn't about regressing—it is about coming as children do: spontaneous, honest, trustworthy seekers who say it like it is. Children are yet to be conditioned to fear, distrust, and forced to see it the adults' way, which many times is not even correct to begin with. It's all likely some person's (past) ego. Ego is the self that you now know. self that you now know is evolving. Your experiences are the teachers. What you do with the experiences is up to you. It is up to you, not others. It is your journey or adventure in life. The self needs to be comfortable with the self. ego role we play on earth is not good or bad, right or wrong, and is not constant. But with each experience, we have a chance to change and grow. Notice, a chance to grow, and if you do not grow with the experience, then you are doomed to repeat the experience. Some people—we all know some—never seem to get it. They just like running into those brick walls. The economy brought down communism, imperialism, and we still don't learn from experiences. That's adolescence. Hopefully, understanding the process will help you choose to change your concepts with experiences to a higher phase of reasoning.

Here is an example of how my reasoning changed. We were taught by the church (others) that Jesus was the *only*-begotten son of God. I had a conflict with this, since the Bible also teaches that we are all sons and daughters of the living God. So now I believe that Jesus was a son of God, a highly-evolved ego (self) enlightened to the point of being selfless. This did not change a thing about my following Jesus, for it is the messages that remain the same. To some this may be blasphemy, but Jesus never declared he was the *only* begotten son. In fact, he tells us in many ways we are and have the same power he has. The Holy Spirit was his teacher, and it is ours. We can still strive to be Christ-like. Virgin really meant back then, first-born of young girl and Jesus was Mary's first-born. This doesn't even change our hymns about the virgin birth of Jesus. You can't grow if you are not willing to look at your conflict. At the pearly gates, there are no excuses except for why you believe what you do. You cannot blame others.

Adolescence is the period between childhood and maturity. Maturity, however, is a lifetime quest. If the US is adolescence at its best, what does this mean? In adolescence, we are to try to find our identity as individuals. It is a period of "it is all about me." It is a defensive and sometimes angry period. It is a time when we do not want to listen to others. It is a paranoid period. The thinking can go like this: "Everyone wants what I have, everyone wants me to be like them, everyone wants something from me, and everyone is out to get me." It is a period of fears of never measuring up and that someone or something is out to get us.

Since the United States is adolescence, each adult or adolescent needs to question everything they were taught. "Who says it's this way or that? Why can't it be this, not that?" You don't need to be confused about where to start, because you start where things just don't ring true. Things that have always given you some uneasiness, maybe a contradiction. What will happen is that you will start to take ownership of your beliefs. Our adolescents are frustrated because reasoning is more or less taken from them. Look, we are just getting around to admitting that we did not record history correctly. It was slanted to make the white Anglo-Saxon Americans feel justified in what we did in our country. Someone had to stand up and be brave enough to say it was time to confess the errors. Thinking for yourself is not in vogue for us, but this is a good time to start. There are two kinds of people in the US: the living and the walking dead. The living are those who choose to grow and learn, and the walking dead are those who let circumstances toss them to and fro.

One out of every five people in the US is depressed or anxious. The walking dead, because they are not directing their own lives, cannot find happiness until they start to be willing to change the way they see things around themselves. It won't be accomplished until they stop being led and blaming others or things outside themselves. Just keep following the "same old, same old" will just get you what you have. If you don't like it, then change it. There is lots of fear in the unknown, but that fear can be changed with loving the challenge. Loving the challenge is zest for life. Most of our population doesn't even realize we are a totalitarian government, which is defined as doing what others want us to do.

The patriot act that our government has passed has nothing to do with being patriotic or democracy. First, it a deep sign of government paranoia, and secondly, it is about control. This author is patriotic in every ounce of her being and genetics. Her being is a descendent of John Irish, Pilgrim in 1629.

Rules and laws are for those who cannot see without them. Others don't need them because they are in the "light." The "light" means being fully aware or enlightened. Light can also mean love, for the best possible person anyone can be is love. "Fully human, fully alive" means knowing your purpose and the meaning of life. There are human laws and there are universal laws. Human laws limit, and universal laws reveal infinite possibilties and freedom. The US has a lot of growing to do, and with each of us taking responsibility for our own growth and development, we will have a better chance of becoming.

The purpose of life is to become all you can become. As stated before, you are born with potential. It is your job as an adult especially to pull that potential out of yourself. You do this by usings your experiences as your teachers. Let's say you are experiencing anxiety (fears). Let's again say it's the fear of failure. Introspection is the step needed now. Ask yourself, "Where do my expectations come from?" Do you own these expectations, helping you to see if they are from within or outside yourself. If from within, meaning you own them, then you would proceed to become more realistic about your owned expectations. It might go something like this: "I need to lighten up, have more fun with my experiences, making them more of a joy than a chore. After all, learning should be fun, and mistakes are learning, growing experiences.

Now, if your fears are all about what others expect of you, you don't own them. You are letting others have control over you, and that will produce anxiety until you take charge of your life. You may want to look at people-pleasing and the need for approval.

Do you need to people-please in order to get validation? Who needs to validate whom? Remember, it is self-esteem, not other esteem. Self-esteem is self's view of self. You do not need validation outside yourself. We should learn this in adolescence, but since the US is adolescence at its best, then thinking you will get a good sense of self out there is futile. Empowerment comes when you own your feelings and fears. The fears or anxiety then can be reduced by not taking yourself so seriously and getting real about your expectations.

Thebody has only so many ways of speaking to us. Our feelings are primary. When you experience depression, anxiety, or any derivative of these feelings, your body is trying to tell you something. The feelings will change when you pay attention to them and figure out what needs to be changed. Our instinct is to just want them to go away. Taking a drug can do this, but it won't change anything but the symptoms. Stay with the feelings, and be positive about the impending learning through change. The human being is all about change. You couldn't stay an infant; you couldn't stay a preschooler or adolescent or stop any aging. Do not try; you were meant to move along. Welcome the feeling. Stay with the feeling, as it is your friend for growth. Introspection time; go inside and see what the feelings are all about. Now, anxiety is about our fears, and depression is about the lack of action in our lives. Action can be translated also as change needed. The change can be minor or major, but one thing we know: it's necessary.

Let me share "Risk" with you. I thought this was Leo Buscaglia's, as he used it some, but the author is unknown. There is more to it than I will share now.

Risk

To love is to risk not being loved in return

To live is to risk dying

To hope is to risk despair

To try is to risk failure

But risks must be taken,

Because the greatest risk in life is to risk nothing.

Tie people who risk nothing do nothing,

have nothing, are nothing, and become nothing.

They may avoid suffering and sorrow,

But they simply cannot learn to feel, and change,

and grow, and love, and live.

Only the people who risk are truly free.

Anonymous

"LOVE YOUR NEIGHBOR AS YOURSELF"

You must first love yourself before you can love your neighbor. You may have been taught that everyone comes before you. But as you can see, loving self is a prerequisite for the love of anyone or anything else. Once you have a sense of self, a good healthy self-esteem, you are then ready to move in the world, detached. It won't be "What's in for me? but "What is the best for the situation or circumstance?" You'll want to do the right thing for the right reasons. Before, we might have done the right thing for the wrong reason. Example: I loved God because I was afraid not to. Now I love because he's my best friend and I have no fear. Detachment is so accentual in the process of becoming. As long as you are ego-bound, you will be attached. Attached to the results or outcome of situations or circumstances. Look again at "Risk," and notice how the attachment to outcome keeps you from becoming. Freedom comes when we are not attached to the outcome. You have experienced expectations for events and been disappointed. Now, think of that event and have no expectations. Can you see how just letting something take its course might be more enjoyable? If two people have each an agenda Lois B. Mayette for an event, then there will be either a conflict or compromise needed. If one says, "1 don't care," then that person's agenda turns out to be a detachment, not caring what the outcome is. They perhaps just enjoy the event. Detachment isn't compliancy—it's freedom. Attachments keep us focused in the wrong places. We look to others or things to make us happy. It is a vicious circle that really can never satisfy. There is never enough. We always want bigger and better. We call this our material phase. Don't apologize if that's where you are now, as

18

over half of our culture is in this phase. The materialistic phase will never be successful in making you happy, since it has a quest in the realm that cannot satisfy. Happiness with things is short-lived. Lasting happiness is deep inside you.

Detachment, again, isn't not caring or neglecting self. It's just the opposite: it is being very involved in worthwhile issues and for the right reasons. The greatest truth is that all suffering originates from desires. So having no expectations frees you for enjoying the flow. When I go to do something with others, if it's a group, if it has to be my way, I'll be very upset when it doesn't work out as I wanted it to. So you can see we can't all have it our way. So going with the flow is what is needed. If something happens that wasn't counted on, you have a choice to be angry or make the best of a bad situation. When in 1992 in Austria skiing, I blew out my knee the first day of skiing. I partook of everything I could for the next twelve days: what else was there to do? I recall being told by the group at the get-together when we got home that they had never seen anyone make the most of the situation as I did. I didn't know at the time what to make of that statement. I am from a family of nine siblings. You have to learn early how to deal with going with the flow. If ego is in check, we do the right things for the right reasons. Your involvement will have purpose and meaning for the whole, rather than just for ego or recognition. Your satisfaction will come from the pure standpoint of advancing the human conditions. Do not minimize this satisfaction of advancing the human condition. It is definitely enough to get high on. High on life satisfaction. Detachment helps us rejoice as a whole when the condition of humans has moved ahead toward fullness and growth. Detachment is not complicity; it's really a natural high all the time. It is the peace that passes all understanding. It is the gut level, it is the heart level, and it is love-level high. It is every cell in your body high. Bottle this, and there would be no diseases. The contented happy chemistry of the body would always be present, and diseases would have nothing to feed upon. Your immune system will ward off a cold, even with someone in your face with a cold. Remember, stress causes most of our disorders.

The ego creates attachment to maintain a sense of selfhood and safety. person who's going places and growing is one who takes risks. Letting go of attachments helps us transcend and be carried beyond the ordinary to the broad, vast unity. There is no separation between self, the world and God (spirit). Most important is that detachment means less caring about the outcome, and therefore the outcome is more readily accepted.

IMAGINATION

Imagination is more important than knowledge.
Albert Einstein

Imagination is defined as the power of the mind to form mental concepts. Imagination can be one of most powerful tools of the mind. We have all had a vivid imagination from our early years. We have all pretended to be someone we are not or have dreamed of a different life and how we would handle it. So, dream of the highest person you would like to be, then make it come to pass. All tools can be used for good or not good, but with owning our choices and responsibilities, let's choose good for our own sake. My fortune cookie said, "They can because they thought they could." Active imagination was being utilized there. Remember those fears that never came to pass? They felt real to you until you decided they were not. Active imagination, again, at work. If you want to be courageous, then act as if you have courage. If you lack confidence, act as if you have confidence. Mind games? No, if it is not there, it would not work, so it was there all the time. Imagination is so important when dealing with change and fears. "Just act as if..." is a tool used to help you get through doubt and build self-esteem.

I use self-hypnosis to center down and relax. Imagination is very important in self-hypnosis and any other relaxation technique. Imagining you are in a meadow of flowers, looking up at the sky with the sun on your skin, takes fantasy and imagination. Put fantasy or imagination to good use. You are not lying to yourself if you use a tool to get where you can; you are facing the issue by acting more positive. I think I can, so therefore, I can. It was there all the time. The tool of fantasy can allow you to explore or employ new responses and avenues. You create for yourself new patterns in thinking, feeling and behaving. Fantasy has truths in it. If someone fantasized a hundred years ago that we would walk on the moon, we would have labeled them insane. Then someone dreamed we would someday walk on the moon, and then someone made it become a reality. That is the process of ideas and reality.

BODY, MIND, AND SPIRIT

We need to take a holistic approach to process, becoming all we can become. It is a process with no time-space necessity. Culturally, we find it hard to have patience, especially with ourselves. process is about patience with perseverance, if you will. You want not to get discouraged but persevere. We all did and do get discouraged. Did you ever think your requests and prayers have gone unanswered? Been there, done that! Remember, we live in time. Growth asks you to let go of time. In order to do this, you need to focus only on your journey and not on where someone else is on theirs. Culturally, we reflect on what others say is so. Growth of self asks us to stop doing that. It is about finding your own voice, taking ownership of your beliefs. Culturally, many do not care about the truth, potential, or purpose. If "the truth will set us free," we need to quest for the truth. That's the process. It becomes free to be me. In the process, there should be no competitiveness, no comparisons, just inside you. Your potential that you were born with.

Potential means what you are capable of becoming, not a wish list, but utilizing that which was the possibilities from birth. It is claimed that we use 10% of our brain (now maybe 12%), and 10% of our talents. It is also known that we do not know that much about the wiring of the brain. We are discovering new ideas all the time. It was just recently acknowledged that the left brain and the right brain cross over more than thought. Some tasks activate both sides of the brain.

An article some time ago talked about nuns of the Order of Notre Dame, living in Minnesota, that were the best Jeopardy players as well as other quiz games. They are a teaching order, they do not retire until age seventy-five, there are about a hundred and fifty in the order, and it is not unusual for over five of them to be one hundred years of age. There is known dementia or Alzheimer's disease. How do they do it? If a topic comes up that they do not know, they divide up the task of learning about it, then come together to teach each other. Also important was that they encourage each other to remain physically active. So they use the total: body, mind, and spirit activation. Their brains have been studied after death and have been known to weigh more than normal. We are reading more and more about challenges and activity of left and right brain warding off Alzheimer's. This shows us again the power of the brain and thinking. It also might put more credence in the saying, "If you do not use it, you lose it."

The body needs physical exercise, the right diet and plenty of rest or sleep. The body houses the mind and spirit. If you are physically in pain, it can certainly drain the energy and cause the mind and spirit to focus on the pain and stop the balance of energy. Balance is necessary so that healing can take place, or so you do not get sick or out of balance to begin with. I refuse to be sick; how? I have not been to a doctor in thirty-three years. My first experience with the mind-pain connection was when I wanted to walk with my husband on his routine walk. He always had a weight problem, so diet and exercise were important to him. He had been fast walking around our neighborhood, and I felt that if I wanted some quality time with him, I could walk with him. He informed me that he was glad for the company but that I would have to keep up, as he wanted to keep the pace that he was used to. I have always been a very active outdoor person—skating, golfing, hiking—and everyone always asked me to slow down when they had to walk with me, so I did not think I would have a problem. Off we went, and after about one half-mile, I started to get leg pains. That was a bummer, as my pride would not let me tell him that I was in pain. So I prayed, "God, if you want me to fellowship with my husband in this way, you will have to help me with the pain." With that, the pain went away. Before you say "luck" or "coincidence," I will tell you, I was so surprised, and I tested it several times after that, and each time pain left. Thirty years later, it still does. This happening back then also helped me quest more for the mind-body-spirit connection. You cannot get what I've got, as it is the process. You need to be willing to learn and change old beliefs. If you do not believe it is possible, then it isn't. And it isn't just a mind thing; it needs to be a whole-being belief. Example: I do not have health insurance. If I got health insurance, I would be telling my psyche that I did not believe anymore that I can heal myself. "Physician, heal thyself." Do not say "I am not a physician"; everyone is. Okay, if you do not want to believe that, then do not. I believe, simple as that. The quest will be there until I draw my last breath on this plane and the one beyond.

This is my take: the soul, with the mind as the power, acts through the endocrine glandular centers to produce the physical conditions. Our Creator intended none of us to be sick. You first need to believe in every cell in your body that you were not meant to be sick. Every cell in your body has a mind, so make sure you are sure you were not meant to be sick. Secondly, your being ill is not punishment, but the lack of understanding the grand scheme of things. The connection of everything to everything, the body, mind, and spirit intention. As I understand this more and more, I desire to do good things for my body, mind and spirit.

Stress is the cause of most of our disorders, physical, mental, and spiritual. Stress needs to be kept at a healthy level. Stress can be reduced with thinking—how we perceive the event or situation. Cognitive (thinking) therapy is used today with great success. Change the way you think and you change the way you feel and behave. Culturally, we are very negative, so you need to reduce the environmental negative input in your life. Remove that negative energy, and your way of dealing with life will no longer be filtered through that negativity. Feelings are the language of the soul, and the soul is never negative. For the soul to grow, which is love, you need to process love. Forgiveness is a good example here. Until you forgive someone or something in your life, you are living outside the soul in that situation. The process for making sense of our wounds is a very personal one, but a common theme in wound healing, according to Joan Borysenko, is the universal need to forgive. If we do not forgive ourselves for our mistakes and others for the wounds they have inflicted on us, we end up crippled with guilt. And the soul cannot grow under a blanket of guilt, because guilt is isolating, while growth is a gradual process of reconnecting to ourselves, to others, and to a greater whole. In our environment, the government, media, and our churches are primarily negative. So take them in small doses; be informed, but if you need to read a paper, the Sunday one has all the week's news. You may not get the truth, but you will be informed nevertheless.

You need to know yourself enough to know what works to reduce your stress. Exercise is good; relaxation techniques are also good, and there are many different kinds of relaxation techniques: yoga, meditation, prayer, or just being still for a period of time. My version of all these I call self-hypnosis. Breathing is primary in all of them: the breath of life, breathing life into yourself. Oxygen is vital to life, both inside and outside the body. Reducing stress is centered around breathing. You feel good after exercise, as you have increased your oxygen in the blood. Smoking deprives your body of oxygen, for it takes up space in the blood. It is not so much about being a sin as it is that it deprives you of good health. Not eating appropriately is the same: you lack balance in fuel to operate well with. Much has been said about persons in the US being overweight. It ties into our unhappiness and instant gratification. Eating, buying, and sex are probably the most-used substitutes for a sense of wellbeing. In our culture, the economy is the driving force. These are all adolescent traits that are prevalent in our culture. It is a false sense of security if you think you're doing well economically and that things are all right. If you are not paying attention to what is going on in the world and around you, the truth, then you are easily lured into the false sense of security. You need to be aware of more than self. Enlightenment is even more important, as it is the absence of ego or self. Ego is the self you know now that wants what it wants and can be selfish, and "the self" is the part of you do not know yet, or the higher self. Deception is defined as a double-dealing. That is neat! You think it is one thing, and it is another. Materialism is supposed to make you happy, but it cannot. The life of something new is short-lived, even new relationships, if you're in it for yourself. We say the honeymoon lasts one to three years, and then reality sets in. If it is your second or third relationship in one to three years, you end up where you were in the last one, because you took your old self into it. So if you have not changed from the end of one relationship to the next, how can this one be different? We are the cause of our own demise. Materialism is blinding, distracting, and deceiving. Bigger, better, or more will not be the seat of happiness. Happiness is contentment and peace of mind. The fearless soul becomes abiding peace. It is a soul journey—not religion, soul! Soul is all of your possibilities, the essence of you. The church is just the foundation, and for the most part a good one, but you can go to church all your life and never find the spiritual self.

Today, churches mainly preach about historical Jesus. Maybe that is all they can do. But that is just the beginning, like the born-again experiences you hear about. It is just the beginning of your quest for or the desire to know God through Jesus, if you are

Christian. All religions have an experience that is an awakening. Then the rest is a lot of hard work, but very rewarding and worth the struggle that follows. What follows is very exciting, mind-boggling, rewarding, mystical, and natural at the same time. Fear keeps us stuck in the historical Jesus and never moving to the spiritual or mystical growth. It is easy to get stuck in the historical realm, as there are so many unknowns that can easily produce fear if you are negative or believe that you are not to know this realm. It is all part of the process of getting to know yourself through knowing Jesus in you or God in you. Jesus is the higher self in you. God is the higher self in you.

John wrote or had the experience of Revelations at the end of his life, and it became the end of the Christian Bible. That is significant, because it is at the end of self that God can come in and through us. I am not making age relevant here, as we are asked to come as little children. Little children are not yet conditioned to be self-conscious and afraid of their consciousness, are free to see and say it like it is. Adults either get afraid of being different, get stuck in dogma, or are just too much of the world yet. They are unable to be open anymore to the spirit of being. If you believe that we are human beings having a spiritual experience, you are ready for spiritual Jesus. The church, like others (the church is just others), does not have the answers for you; you have the answers for you and you alone. It is helpful to see that the process of becoming all you can become is inside you, and you have to pull it out of yourself. You need to trust yourself. You will know if it is not the truth. If you do not know right away, you will if you keep forging ahead. Remember, what you likely knew as your truth yesterday is always evolving. Example: "God is fear," then "God is love," then "God is unconditional love." See the progression? It is nothing to fear. fear of God becomes the awesomeness of God. Take it even further: "I am in God and God is in me." You can find that in the

Bible. God is, after all, spirit. If you are Christian, you are trying to become Christlike. The Muslim is in the same light—they are trying to be like Mohammed; the Hindu, a follower of Krishna; etc. You can think, if you want to, that God made a mistake when he placed each of us in our faith, but I believe he did not make a mistake in my culture, my religion or my parents. Of course, I believe further that he did not do this to me or choose this for me, but that I choose it in order to advance my spirit. See how our beliefs can evolve over time? My journey is still evolving. I must learn—it is my high on life. I am soul, which is not connected to matter or material. Well, I am working on that; some days are better and closer to soul then others. Some days, I am just flesh.

Because of the presence in us of the spirit, we can, after processing and getting the knowledge of how it works, fix our intellectual sights on the realities of the unseen worlds; and, in the knowledge of them, know both what is true and how to believe. This result is not easily obtained. Ask, and you shall receive directions, as not everyone goes down the same path the same way. Some go to groups, because they learn best there; some go to college or school; some read about others' journey to get ideas of how to journey; but the last word is yours. Processing will involve not only immense intellectual effort, including the repeated challenging of assumptions, but also turning your back on everything in life that is merely material. In other words, you need to be ready and serious about giving attention to this phase of you life.

How could we have believed in a God of fear? As loving mothers and fathers, we should never want our children to fear us; respect, love, but not fear. I think it got translated incorrectly and was distorted for power and control. Not God's need for power or control, but the need of religious leaders and rulers. It should be today, an awesome God. God loves us unconditionally This translates really into absolutely, without limits, and naturally. Not right or wrong, good or bad, lovable or unlovable, but unconditionally. The awesomeness of God is steadfast and consistent: therefore, he is always working for the good in us to come out. He always looks out for our best interests, so when trials come along, it is not about right or wrong or good or bad; it is about learning and growing. God sees us as a loving parent should see their children, as working out our own lives. It is not right or wrong; it is just the way we need to experience a situation in order to learn and grow.

Bad things happen to good people for a good reason: so that we can learn and grow. There are not good or bad people—there are people who are refusing to learn their lessons in life. Being bad does not get you what you need. It may get you what you want but not meet your needs. We all need contentment and peace of mind. Being bad does not get you that. It gives you restlessness and leaves you unsatisfied. Love is the answer with no fear—unconditional love. We thrive on love. All things thrive on love. It is culturally more prevalent to use fear in this country than love. It is likely because we have been a patriarchal society, and our society is quickly changing.

"Love one another as I have loved you" is a necessity. Fear tactics are used in our government, the media, medicine, and education. Greed, not love, is the reason. Greed will never give you peace of mind. Money, power, and control are the deceptors. You know that the more you have, the more you have to lose. I believe our economy is about to collapse, as it should. It is been on the wrong road for too long. We need something to turn us toward love and caring. Four years ago, I thought we could turn ourselves around. Hopi Indians, whom I admire, say it is now too late, and I agree with them. This does not stress me out, however, and the reason is that I'm the soul. You can kill the body, but not the soul. If a child is going down the wrong road, action needs to be taken. Action is needed in our culture to get us back to basics:

love, caring, and sharing. We are an arrogant, greedy, and self-centered society. This is not a scolding; rather, it is a warning, so that when it happens you will not be caught off guard, as many will. After all, how do we move from a culture of adolescence to at least young adulthood? It will take some rude awakening. What sad is this has been written about for over forty years, and changes have not occurred. One of my college professors, some time ago, claimed that we were on the brink of disaster because we were borrowing from Peter to pay Paul for too long. What happens if you do that in your budget? Where do you think your 401K and pensions are?? I know you think they are safely put away for safekeeping. Oh, no—they are gone, for the most part. How come your 401K went down in this bad economy instead of even staying as it was? When we crash, we all go down together except for those who put money in the EURO. We are an arrogant people, meaning proceeding from an undue claim of self-importance.

On March 6, 1992, I was in München, Germany when Mikhail Gorbachev was there to promote his newly-written book. I had blown out my knee on the first day of skiing, so I did not want to do a lot of walking and went to the Hofbrauhaus where I was to meet the rest of the ski group at four p.m. Security was very tight, and they would not let me in that early. I stood outside in a group for over three hours. Gorbachev was late, as I believe he was due at three p.m. Next to me in the crowd was an Italian female physicist, and on the other side was a female from California who worked for Radio Free Europe. We talked for three hours on the direction the United States was going. They were very aware and on target, so there was no need for me to disagree with them. Now this is some thirteen years ago and I can say the same thing today. We just do not get it. We are just regressing so fast that all of us had better take notice, and if we cannot do anything about our government, we had better do something about our own lives to be ready for the fall. I do not believe in fall of the world, but I believe that powers come and go. Today, we are buying like crazy from China, and then borrowing from her to pay her. Talk about having our act together. But that is adolescence. It is said that our government has us so busy working to pay the bills that there is no time or energy left for protesting what is going on. I do not believe we do not know what is going on; I believe that it all looks too big for the little guy to do anything about it. Our personalities are weak; we do not have any fight left in us. Our mentality needs to change, and that brings us back to the process. You need to see that it is very important to stretch our perspective on issues— issues like people. Humans are more important than things.

Let us get back to understanding that humans, no matter where they live or what they believe, are all God's children. Until you can believe we are all one, you do not get it. We are all body, mind, and soul. We are all one under God, the same God, and our religious beliefs are all basically the same. There are fundamentalists in all religions, and one of the personality traits of fundamentalists is that they just want to be important. Now is not that sad, that we make our brothers and sisters feel so unimportant that they have to be radical? All religions talk about the sacredness of human life. Love is what we need to process toward in order to see all people, regardless of race, color, or religion, as our brothers and sisters. Difference is beauty, or we would not be created different. Every time you are refusing to see this, you are denying God. He created all of us. Why would there be favorites? That would not be unconditional love, which God is. Greed, power, control and lust are issues that need to be examined by each of us as we process. God is constant, so he is not favoring Christ over Mohammed or Buddha. The messages of all are beautiful. I highly recommend you study other religions. I am not religious, but I am spiritual. To me, they are day and night. Again, you can go to church all your life, but spirituality is personal: the issues of you and your potential. Your potential is God's gift to you. But he has that same gift for everyone. It is just that we are all different; therefore, he meets us where we are at. So you are what you believe, and that is honored by God. Let us honor others where they are at, and not where we want them to be. There is a strong need to have people validate you; we want them to agree that we are right. In the process, this has to go, as, truthfully, you need to validate yourself. We all have work to do on earth, or we would not be here. We are working out our own spiritual growth.

First, let us look at the healthy human being, no matter where they live. It is said that they are androgynous, meaning having the characteristics of both sexes. It can also mean flexible in either role. Now, it has little to do with what you have between your legs. It has to do with your thinking, feelings, and attitude. Women and men who see themselves fitting either role are less likely to ascribe tasks as either female or male. Try see a task, and if can do it, they just do. It is not a female task or a male task. Now, we have made progress in the last five or so years in our culture in ascribing roles. Example: military, doctors, lawyers, merchants, and chiefs. We as of yet have not had a female president, and many countries have had females heads of state.

In Eastern cultures, there has been strong fostering of the yin and yang concepts for both male and female. That is the developing of both sides of your personality, the male and female. If you are female, then you need to develop the male side, and if male, you would develop the female side. Then you would be androgynous and whole. You would think and feel less about your being male or female. The respect for both would increase. Our cultural stumbling block has been the lack of belief in reincarnation. If Jesus came again, what would it be called? Jesus would be reincarnated. It would be the reincarnate Jesus. Jesus and his disciples believed in reincarnation; read Matthew 17:1-

13, the story of the transfiguration. The church leaders tried to erase reincarnation from the people for more control and used fear as the basis for much of the Christian beliefs. This was done two hundred to five hundred years after Jesus. Reincarnation makes sense, and having one chance to get it all right does not. So whether you are male or female now, believe me, you have been the opposite sex many times before, so get used to it. Try to remember what it felt like to be the opposite now, as you will advance much faster. It makes sense to develop your yin and yang. Yin is the opposite of Yang, though they are interdependent. Yin can be the moon, yang the sun. In China, they believe, they balance each other. This gives you the idea of all being energy and interdependent and flowing together. If one was not there, then the other would not be there. They make up the whole. Now, develop that which is already within you.

With the liberation of the gay and lesbian community, that is for the gay and lesbian men and women to be honored in our society, a larger definition of masculinity and femininity has to happen. The larger definition, which includes many more forms of masculinity and femininity, will in the end help the straight community as well. is because homophobia really is gender police. If a straight man, let's say, feels something and shows emotions, often his friends will say, "Stop being so gay," or "Do not act like a sissy." This keeps men boxed in so that they cannot be connected to their full range of emotions. So as society gets more comfortable with the gay and lesbian community; straight men and women will ultimately have the opportunity to be comfortable in their own skin.

Let us look again at the United States and see just how far we have to go to get even with other cultures. We still have not had a female president, when nations in many parts of the world have had women leaders. Women are partly to blame for where they are, as they have been too comfortable being taken care of and not being assertive. There are more women voters than men, so we cannot cop out there. Men in our culture feel trapped emotionally. They cannot express their full selves. It is not totally their fault, as we had the John Wayne macho mentality for a long time, and a lot of resistance in changing it. Boys do not cry, so they therefore shut out their feelings. "Do not be a sissy' is still being voiced by dads who are afraid of their own masculinity or question their own masculinity. So how can males in US get started on the process of becoming all they can become? Their view of masculinity is a good place. Be honest with your feelings. How do you feel if you were to cry in public? In February of 1987, Reader's Digest had an article about crying. Thee title was, "Why Do We Feel Good After We Cry?

It went on to say that with every type of tear, there were different types of hormones secreted. It seems that crying helped balance the chemical makeup of the body and helped persons feel good or better, concluding that crying is good for you. Males not being in touch with their feelings has backfired in many ways in our country. Their outlets for this lack have been known mostly in the aggressive behaviors like rape, drinking, drugs, and general sexual attitudes. Entrapped emotions have left their energy to go to libido or anger. %ere is a lot of anger in our males. It is right on the surface, and they confuse it with emotional fears. It is squashed down for fear that if it gets out, they will not be able to get back in control. Have you noticed that women do not cry as much as they used to? Well, they have a lot more control over their lives and are stronger. If we could get our males to get there, they would feel much better, having more outlets to express themselves. Men confuse sex with love. Sex may be a part of love, or may be selfishness, but it is not necessarily love. Males feel something powerful in sex, and it the most powerful feeling they have, so it must be love. Wrong—it is likely just energy relief that feels good. The art of lovemaking is like life: it is always being learned. It is not something that comes naturally, really; it is learned by communicating about it. God forbid we discuss likes and dislikes—we may learn something. Half the men in US are likely still having premature ejaculation, too afraid to ask for help, when help is so simple. Tie new epidemic is porno. Talk about disrespect for personhood. There it is, and the reason is the lack of knowing the art of lovemaking. An art is enough in and of itself, especially if you are good at it. Males are afraid they are missing out on something, and they are; the art of lovemaking. I'm not saying that sometimes you do not need to use creative imagination in lovemaking, but not fantasy to the point of disrespect for others. Porno is big business in the US, and our government really does not want to creek down on anything that is big business today with the economy so much in trouble. You can also see that it is mostly a male government, and many of them have a problem with keeping their penises in the right place. Men are really whores. Now, there are some males who have it together. They just need to help their counterparts get to a healthier and happier place. Men are bored and lack meaning in their lives, since they are always guarded. The more involved with life you are, the more meaningful life becomes. Involved, but not meaning just keeping busy for the sake of being occupied, but involved with whatever is around you. Challenge yourself with something you have never tried. You will learn more about yourself. Start letting your emotions come to the surface in love, rather than anger, control, or aggression. You never have to fear your emotions of love. You really cannot love too much. See where sex and your attitude about sex lie. Women do not have low libidos—they are just busy giving love to everything they do, and therefore their satisfaction levels are spread out over many areas. Females get lots of satisfaction from giving to others and really need to take a little more for themselves. They are getting better at that. Females need to see sex less as just for love and romantic aspects and know that it has other functions. Like an energy balancer, reassurance stabilizer, and just because they want to.

Tiere are more and more in our culture who are on the awareness trail, and that is the good news, as I do not want to sound like the whole country is oblivious to the meaning of life. There are some good writers today saying the same thing that is being said here, just from different or their perspective. Victor Frankl has what he describes as existential vacuum.

That feeling, of which so many persons complain today, of namely the feeling of the total and ultimate meaninglessness of their lives.

This meaninglessness comes many times, when you are basically stuck. But this is good, because it is your being telling you that you need a challenge. You are bored with the same old, same old. People are more important than things. So the challenge might be finding a need in someone else and filling it. That feels good, and that is love, caring and sharing. Branch out find another need and fill it; do not get stuck. Change what you believe, and you will change your behavior. Again, the power of thinking is primary. Our bodies have just so many ways of talking to us. Meaninglessness and boredom really result in depression. Half our nation could likely be diagnosed as depressed. Depression is the body's way of saying, "Add a new dimension to your life." Being stagnant will cause depression. Be willing to grow and learn. Think outside your box. Leave your comfort zone. Become again and again and again. There may be no end to your potential. Every time I have a fear of something, I challenge myself to overcome the fear. That is what it is there for. I have been doing that since I was a little girl, and I look back and have no idea how I knew enough to go into my fears. I was very shy as a youngster, and after graduating from high school, I took that shy little girl by Greyhound bus to Missouri, to airline school, from the farm in upstate New York. Then I went to work for Eastern Airlines. Talk about challenges and throwing myself into the world at eighteen and nineteen. I still go into my fears and conquer them, as avoidance is your worse enemy. By avoiding, you learn nothing. Take one fear and conquer it. Fears are not good or bad; they want to be your teachers.

I am going to give you my take on the parable of the talents or gold coins (Luke 19:11-27). First, note the two words used for what was given: gold coins and talents. Now, the definition for "talent" is twofold. It is the gold coin of ancient times and it is the talents, your potential given at birth. Now, a man of high rank was going away to be king and gave his ten servants each a gold coin and told them to earn or increase the amount. When he returns, as they knew he would, we then learn about what three of his servants did to increase the talents. One earns ten coins from the one given, and the king gave him charge of ten cities; the next one earned five and was given charge of five cities; and the last hid his gold coin out of fear. My first impression is of Jesus saying, "I am going away, so that you might get the teacher, the Holy Spirit." Thenext important impression is the word "talents." And the third is about increasing the talents. Okay, you figured out where I am going with this. Good. You are given talents, and your job is to increase them. It is not about staying safe and fearful; it is about thinking outside the box. I would rather have you hot or cold than lukewarm or safe. No risks in lukewarm. Search for the answers, the truth about yourself, and it will be found. That is what life is: searching and finding new ideas and concepts. Some people have the born-again experience, and that is all well and good, but it is just the beginning. %ere are a lot of searching and risks to now be taken in order to grow and learn the truth. I call the born-again experience "the first principles." You have a direction and maybe a passion; now do the journey. The first principles are the laws. It is a long journey to grace, or becoming Christlike, if that is your choice. If you are Buddhist, Hindu, or Muslim, awareness is the first step, and then the journey to nirvana. Muslims seek *tawhid*, or oneness with God. The heart of Islamic life is the degree in which one becomes tawhid or the oneness with God. The call of Islam, therefore, concerns, above all, the remembrance of a knowledge deeply embedded in their being, the confirmation of knowledge that saves, hence the soteriological (saving) function of knowledge in Islam. You say "Yes," down deep in your soul where the knowledge was all the time. Is not that the same as the awakening in the born-again experience in the Christian faith? God is the God of all; he has no favorites or special people. He will lead you to the greater truth if you will just seek the truth. Remember, Jesus' greatest teachings were against the current beliefs of the time; he went against the church leaders. The ignorance of the truth is the cause of all misery, according to Buddha. Alvars is one who is immersed in God-love.

GROWTH OF THE SOUL: LOVE

I sat on the porch one summer afternoon and watched a spider make its web. It did not make its web design as I expected. It made the web very irregularly. I tried to figure out a rational pattern for its movements, but there just did not seem to be one; it was literally going all over the place. But the spider must have had a plan, for when it was finished, the web was perfectly symmetrical. I thought of God and his creation. We sometimes feel that God's design in our lives makes little sense. We live, we suffer, we grow, and then we die. But life does make sense, and it is a perfect design. As I look at my life, everything fits so well in place. Each experience leads one closer to the truth. It is a spiritual truth; love. The spider labored to create a web, so as to catch his food. I labor to create the best possible me I can be. Our experiences do not just happen; we need them to happen so we can grow and learn. Each is a thread that helps me remember who I am. We are spiritual beings having a human experience. The experiences are the keys to learning, or remembering, more about our purpose and the meaning of our lives.

Experiences make you more aware. Awareness the key to perfection. Not ego (self), but spiritual perfection, the self. It is not about the body—it is about the spirit of the body. The spirit in this body, as well as around the body, and its connection to the bigger body of spirit we call God, the universal Spirit. We are one, we are here, we are there, we are one with God. You can feel this more as you move into the truth. The truth will set you free, not separate. All religions teach at the center of their beliefs that oneness with God is the goal. We are all on the same journey. "Love one another" is written in all religions as the main theme.

Try loving one another as part of your process; for one month, or one day, act as if everyone is your sister or brother. %ere go competitiveness, greed, corruption, control, power, sexual abuse, whoring around, and wars. Oh! The most important, wars. The selfish, senseless wars, all in the name of God. Obviously, we do not have one God, as everyone believes that God is on their side. Let's try this another way: God is love, God is unconditional love, and God does not have favorites. God wants us to love one another, God created all of us, God loves our differences. God did not make a mistake in his design. He gave us free will; he did not want robots. He wanted us to decide what is the best possible us. Churches are really our problem, because they told us all this, then some churches took it all away from us: "You cannot do this, you can not do that, and this is the only way God will accept you." What a contradiction. Those are the ones that gave me such problems. God is unconditional love. If it does not ring true, *it is not.*

Example: I grew up in a Catholic neighborhood, in the only Protestant family in the neighborhood. At the time, the Catholic church was telling their congregation that the Protestants went to hell (even though there is none). Since, my friends were all Catholics, they were fearful for me, and it gave me some concerns. I went to the Catholic church as much as my Methodist church. My prayers, said every night on my knees, were the Lord's Prayer, Hail Mary, Act of Contrition, and ended with, "and God, I know you are the God of the Protestants too." I said this on my knees from the ages of seven to nineteen. How ignorant is that? My best friend that I grew up with, for years as an adult, would apologize for the church and the things she believed back when we were growing up. We were both caught in a web of lies. She denounced the Catholic church as the result. Now, there is a blessing in all this, as it is a big factor in my quest for the truth. It really shaped me as a thinker.

CHOICES AND RESPONSIBILITIES

There is no hell, lest you make it so. There is no hell, just despair. Do you think love would create a pit (hell) for you to burn in for eternity, or some such belief? Think of a parent creating for their children a no-way-out place of eternal damnation. (That might not be the best analogy, for there are some awful parents.) If you do not get this, close the book. It is because you think it is. It does not make it so—it makes it your belief. You can create anything and make it feel real to you. That does not make it real for others necessarily. There is your truth and my truth, but regardless, the real truth will be followed by the peace that passes all understanding. It is a high-on-life experience. It is a lightbulb experience. You cannot wait to tell someone about the discovery. It is gut-level, it is navel-level, it is center-level and it is solar-plexus-chakra-level. There is no hell, just despair. You create the despair. Oh yes, you do! Take any situation you are in and realize that you choose the situation. Now the real issue is, what do you want to do with this situation? Choices and responsibility are free will. Bottom line: it is up to you to make a difference. If you want to add "with God's help" in Lois B. Mayette this situation, that is fine, for he is already there with you anyway. He is you and you are him, whether you know it or not. He never abandons you or forsakes you. He experiences the situation through you. Now, how do you and he want to experience this situation? He really has no preference, as it would not be free will if he did. I can tell you, if you thought he was in everything you do, as he is, then maybe you would give your choices and responsibility a little more consideration. Well, he's in your bedroom, he's in your kitchen, in your workplace, and everywhere you are. That's because it cannot be any other way. He wants you to be the best possible person you can be, not for his sake but for yours. We feel really good when we do the right thing. There is a dichotomy in this, as he cares and he does not care. In other words, he wants you to use your free will. We should really slow down our reaction time in most situations, and the question should be, "What is the best possible solution for this situation?" The high you get when doing the right thing comes with the peace that passes all understanding. Now, if you decide to go with a selfish solution, that is all right too. If you do not get it this time, then maybe you will the next. You see, time-space does not exist in the spirit realm. There is no wrong or right way. Get this if you can. I have this little prayer when bad things happen to me: "Please do not take this away from me until I have learned all I can from it, as I do not want to repeat this situation." Watch out for what you pray! I already said there is no bad, and I do not like the word, but you get the picture. "Unfortunate situations happening" may be a better term. So, when unfortunate situations happen, they are there to help us experience ourselves. Choices and responsibilities of what you want for yourself. We call them bad because we do not like our feelings, but later, when we look back on them, we can see the value in the experience. There are many tough-love experiences; start to call them that, and maybe it will make your choices and responsibilities easier. God is unconditional love, but tough love too. In the tough-love situations, he does not interfere, but if we want to do the wrong things, even knowing it is wrong, he lets us suffer the consequences. Love has many parts, degrees, and angles, but no conditions. We use tough love on children when they need it and are not getting the point. When we refuse to learn, tough love, even from a friend, is good in retrospect. We are not to leave it up to God. God is in us and we in him. So get on with the task. "Let go and let God" has been misused; however, there is a good time to do that, and that is when we want others to shape up. Let go of what others are doing or being, and do not take their inventory.

If feelings are the language of the soul, then there are no bad feelings. You can stop experiencing them as bad and see the love of learning. Feelings of the soul are love, joy, peace, compassion, and affection. If fears are there as teachers, then the feeling of the soul would be joy. The soul is joyful that you have the opportunity to grow and learn about yourself and what you are capable of. Loving thoughts and actions build good, both internally and externally. Externally meaning the universe and internally meaning the self. It is very important that we see we all make a difference in the whole of the universe too. So when you have a good day, give it away and make a difference. Culturally, we have been taught that everyone else is important but not the self, especially women. As we have come into our own, we realize that we are very important. We make a very good contribution to people around us, but if we are not happy or fulfilled, then we have nothing to give away. Give from your excess and not at your expense. In order to have an excess, you need to see yourself for yourself. Love your neighbor as yourself, but do not neglect yourself. A happy person has everything to give away.

EVERYTHING IS ENERGY

To know that what is impenetrable to us really exists, manifesting itself as the highest wisdom and most radiant beauty which our dull faculties can comprehend only in their most primitive forms—this knowledge, this feeling is at the center of true religiousness. In this sense, and in this sense only, I belong to the ranks of devoutly religious men.

Albert Einstein

If everything is energy, then anything is possible ($E=MC^2$, energy equals mass times speed of light squared). Paradigm shift is needed now; everything is energy. Transcending limitations and old models is what we are now going to talk about. In a sense we have been talking about it, when in becoming all you can become, is asking you to stretch your thinking. New thinking is a paradigm shift. To grow, you need to be willing to comprehend things in new light. Remember, supernatural may be natural, but we just do not understand it yet. God is spirit, I am spirit, you are spirit, spirit is energy. Everything is energy. Subtle energy is the invisible forces that make up the world. Seeing is believing, but the paradigm shift is that seeing is not possible, so you have to believe on faith. Now, test your faith: everything is energy. Look around and see things as energy. We are all one. Everything is connected to everything. If you're sensitive and caring when someone hurts, you hurt to the degree that you relate. We say we feel sorry to express what we feel. What is crying in the movies, even when we do not want to be seen crying? At what level do you think that crying is taking place? The spiritual level—your spirit is recognizing a parallel or past experience. You are not conscious of it, but your spirit, at that moment, is aware. Faith asks us to believe in things not seen, but hoped for. The hope for here is growth and awareness. Life is not about doing—it is about being. Being all you can be, pulling out that potential. It is not possible to disappoint God, for he has no need for you to do life one way or the other, but if it were, I would think that your not using your talents, those known and unknown, would be a way of disappointing him, as it should disappoint you. Stop being the walking dead, if that is where you are, and become more conscious. Welcome a spiritual awakening. Ideas or beliefs move from the subconscious to the conscious by your being ready. Transcending limits means becoming more conscious. It is a spiritual awakening, but spirit is energy. Thinking is the powerhouse; what do you think thinking is? Got it! It is energy. You may think, "I hope no one can read my thoughts," but they are energy, so they are already out there. Collective thinking moves mountains. If we all believed the same thing, as we have already, what we were agreeing on comes true. Be careful of what you want or think—you will get it if you are convinced that you must have it. Here is my take on the walls of Jericho. The walls came tumbling down because they were of one mind. Remember, they went around seven times, and the walls came tumbling down. There was great determination by the seventh time. Think about wars or riots. What fuels the wars, riots, or a mob? It is thought—thinking or beliefs. If they are strong beliefs, they move walls. The walls of Jericho really came tumbling down. The universe is all energy. Energy can be dense and vibrate at a lower level, or it can be air, wind, or spirit and vibrate-at a higher level. You do not see everything vibrating, so you may believe it does not vibrate. You are what you think or believe.

I never believed in the devil (evil yes, devil no). It does not exist for me. If God was omnipotence, omniscience, omnipresence, or any other "omni," then he did not need an adversary. There is enough evil in mankind; we do not need a devil. Remove that negative energy, and your way of dealing with life will no longer be filtered through that negativity. I believe bad things happen to good people for a good reason. I also believe depression, anxiety, and fears are positive, as the body has just so many ways of getting our attention. So we can stop feeling bad if we want and welcome a new adventure with insight and awareness in the wings. If you could maintain a balance of energy in your body, your mind, your emotions, and even your spiritual life, you would not be able to get sick. You would then be vibrating on the physical level on a higher energy plane. Now, before you start to say, "She does not know what she is talking about," I have not been to a doctor in more than thirty years. I have blown out a knee while skiing in Austria (1992) and pulled a hamstring in a leg two years ago. A physical therapist was in my skiing party, and when she saw my knee, a day after it happened, it would not even stay in place and was very swollen. She wanted to get the swelling down, as she said I would have more damage if I did not. I was in great pain, so I welcomed anything that was going to move me forward. She taught me what she called "energy transference." She first demonstrated it to me, and the pain went right away. Then she had me try it, and again, the pain went away. In the night when it hurt, I did the procedure again, and it was magic. Next morning at breakfast, I told Ellie that it worked, and she laughed and said, "How dare you think it would not?' ,Everyone wanted to know more and laughed also. I could not ski the rest of the trip, but I walked and went everywhere they did. She said my knee would take thirteen weeks to heal, and it did. Well, in thirteen weeks it was like new. In fact, in July of that year, I went skiing with the group to New Zealand, with no problem. In 2003, I pulled a hamstring going to vote. Some friends prayed over my leg or knee, and I also used the same energy transference technique. It took longer for it to heal, and this time I had to use crutches for two weeks. It is as good as new, and I have walked eighteen holes of golf four times a week. I have no pain or arthritis in either legs or knees. Remember the elusive energy! I cannot explain what transpired, but it worked. Subtle energy is an invisible force that makes up the world. Ellie said I likely have strong energy in my hands, and that, too, I believe. So maybe just because I believed, it happened. It does not change things, for thoughts are powerful tools. And thoughts are energy. I have used breathing, relaxation techniques, self-hypnosis, and yoga to heal headaches, body pains, insomnia, etc. "Supernatural" may mean just things we do not understand yet. Breath has been associated with life, or life force, for eons. Breath is energy; air is energy; without it you die. But more importantly, making sure you breathe deeply every day is important, as we in this culture are shallow breathers. It is important to increase your lung capacity; ask anyone who has gotten over panic attacks. Deep breathing is a vital part of helping relieve panic attacks, along with dealing with your fears.

When my life passed before me, the general message was to let me know that I already knew everything; now I needed to live it out as if I knew. Free of fears and anxiety, knowing that the purpose of life was to become all I could become by bringing to my consciousness that which we are and becoming one with all things. Potential is in you now; you must pull it out, as no one else can for you. Everything is energy, and everything is conscious. I remember when I did not believe that talking or playing music to your plants helped them grow and thrive. Now I believe it. One of the easiest ways to think about all things being connected is to think of fire. All things burn, and therefore, the product, if they were to burn, is heat or energy. Everything has a melting point. Since we began exploring outer space, this has become more apparent: as our space ships reenter our atmosphere, a heat shield keeps the spaceship from burning up.

I admire the American Indians, because they are very spiritual. I-ley have always understood that everything was energy and we and the universe are one. alone should change your view of things, because remember, you were likely taught that they were savages. Far from it—they helped my relatives survive the winters in Massachusetts in the 1600s. Do you realize that the Indians never tried to convert anyone? helped but did not have a need to make you like them, because their spiritual beliefs were so much like what is needed today. The American Indians recognized the beauty in differences. So they did not need you to agree with them. Today, the Christian religion believes everyone has to be a Christian. So they set out to change others who do not believe as they do. Wrong, we need to recognize God's plan: that some be Hindu, some Buddhist, some be Muslim, and some be Christian, and that we all respect each other's beliefs. Control, power, and even greed were at the root of needing people to agree that there was one true religion. If you felt good about yourself, then you would see that there is no need to have affirmation from others. You would conclude that everyone is of God and a unique individual. In fact, you would see that everyone walking the face of the earth today is a unique, important individual. Remember, no two are alike. Differences are beauty. You could not choose this or that if there was not a choice. It is all about choices and responsibility. You know what happened to my narrow-mindedness after reading and studying other religions? I could now embrace each religion as valid and admire the beliefs and history, because their beliefs were basically the same as the Christian beliefs. Their history was very important, because it was easy to see a need at the time, for a moving forward in the beliefs of the time. Someone needed to speak out, so a new prophet was born to help the people move ahead. In fact, Jesus was just that: he spoke out in his time against some of the old laws and ways. Remember how upset the Sadducees and Pharisees were at Jesus' teachings. God did not die 2005 years ago, although most Christians act as if he did. God forbid (God's laughing now) we think there are highly evolved prophets among us today.

Prophets and angels are called messengers of God. Now, we can at times all claim to be angels and prophets, as God is not dead and speaks to all of us if we think of it or are willing to listen. We hate silence, so of course, we hate to listen. If you have all the answers, you do not need to. What is the Holy Spirit? Jesus, said, "I go so that you might get the Holy Spirit, your teacher, counselor, and guide." Most churches recognized a Holy Spirit but never taught how to use the Spirit. Most Christians never utilize the Spirit as a guide, teacher, or counselor; therefore, they looked to others for direction and guidance. One church, the Catholic church, almost forbade their congregation from reading the Bible and told them they were not capable of understanding it. How insulting! The Holy Spirit was mouthed but was not looked to for guidance or growth, so progress and growth was very slow for a large part of US Christians.

Control and power, not misunderstanding, was the issue, and sheep to slaughter. For sheep just follow and do not question the teachings. There is the biggest problem: fear of questioning those who think they have the answer for everyone. Some churches' messages had become about giving and not being. It was clear that if you gave, especially to the church, you could buy your way to heaven. This may upset you, but that is my intent. Laugh at what you once believed. When I was a child, the Catholic church made public to the congregation the giving of each family in the congregation. In fact, I can tell you today the name of the family in my hometown who always managed to give the most. It was sad, because on the way home from church, the day it was posted for everyone to see, the conversation was about where you were on that list.

"Never good enough" is not about God. Everyone is a unique, important individual. Big fear about Hell back then. Remember, God meets you where you are at, both then and now. If you did not know any better, his unconditional love still enveloped you. Woe to those who led you astray.

Be comfortable, until you are not, in your beliefs; own them, but realize they are yours and that there is no need for you to expect anyone else to believe as you do. %ere are no two persons or experiences alike. We are all on a journey—ours. is hard to realize, because for centuries, we were told it was not about self. It is your journey. The higher self, that I call "the self," is what you seek. It is always evolving as you find your talents and possibilities. The latest tough experience I had was learning, at 62, to scuba-dive. I am not even a good swimmer. I am still not skilled at it, but I love it, especially in the tropics, where fish are bright and colorful, with surprises all around you. My fear of the water, yet love for it, was tremendous. Go into your fears; do not expect them to go away on their own, as they will not. God is love, not fears.

CHANGING YOUR OLD BELIEFS

Research has shown that in order to change or get rid of old beliefs, the old neuron pathways in the brain, you have to replace them with something else. Old habits die hard! When you override an old belief often enough with the new belief, that old belief literally breaks down, physically and chemically in your brain, so that the old belief loses its control. That is when the new belief has taken over.

Your old beliefs are something like highways in the brain. When you stop using the old beliefs long enough, it is like a highway that has not been driven in a long time, one that gets cracks and fills with weeds and even trees. It is not easy to let go of some of our old beliefs; it takes a lot of hard work and conscious effort, but in the long run, it will be worth it, as at the same time as changing our thinking, we are changing our behavior, the behavior that is no longer working for us.

Research also shows that a subject's view of a problem has an important impact on coping. Participants who felt they could change a situation or choose solutions for change tended to use problem-solving techniques rather than emotional responses. They felt better and more in control.

Now, let us look at how guilt, forgiveness and negativity work in the process of becoming. You own your thoughts, feelings and behavior. *No one* can make you, think, feel or behave; you are choosing to. Taking ownership is very important as we and others have said, "You made me angry," "You made me feel bad," and etc. No, they did not, you chose to think, feel and behave.

Once you take ownership of your behavior, you are half way to changing the situation. Now, let us take guilt. It does not come from God. It is a choice. You will wrestle with guilt when changing old beliefs. Old habits die hard; is not fluff. Guilt always comes when trying to change old beliefs, because you owned the old ones for so long that it is hard to take on a new belief out of fear. If you believed the old for so long, you must have been wrong all the time. Take "You made me angry." You believed for so long that someone else was responsible for your feelings. Now you want to believe they do not make you anything; you are choosing that response. So replace the guilt with the knowledge that you did not understand and now you do. Say, "I am glad I now know." Why is it good that you now know? Because now you can do something about the anger. We cannot change others; we can only change self, and now you are in charge of the thinking, feeling, and behavior. Guilt is the old fighting with the new. You have evolved from believing others or situations cause your anger to your owning it and then being able to do something about it. God does not give you guilt, so you stay stuck blaming others and not becoming the best possible you; he wants you to grow. So you see, the first step in letting go of guilt or anger is the owning of it. Change your thinking, therefore change your feelings, and thus your behavior.

Forgiveness is necessary because not forgiving hurts, really, mainly you. Many times, the ones we do not want to forgive do not even know or care about forgiveness from us. If they do know there is a need to forgive, then it entails them. What if someone is deceased or they are not available to us? We still need to forgive for our sake, so we can put it behind us and move on. The lack of forgiveness really hinders you from moving on with your growth. It can still run your life. To move from victim to survivor, forgiveness is necessary. If you are at fault, then you help others go from victim to survivor. Many persons believe that forgiveness is okaying the act or situation that happened, but it is not, and that is what stops them from forgiving. Make sure you examine why you find it hard to forgive. You may like being the victim. Let's say you were sexually abused. Forgiving the perpetrator is not okaying the act against you. Sexual abuse is still running your life until you come to terms with it, and forgiveness is necessary. If you are a victim, it still runs your life; as a survivor, you can put it behind you. We all can learn from everything that happens to us, if no more than that it should not happen to us or others. Get a voice about sexual abuse, as it runs wild in our culture. You may be able to speak out or get laws passed or get sexuality out in the open more. The lack of understanding in adolescence is the main problem in our culture. Sexuality and respect are the key to good sexual attitudes.

So, forgiveness is really deciding that you are going to dissect the issues and be ready to let go by putting it behind you. Let it be in the past and not the present. Many people do not want to let go, as it has become a way of life to feel sorry for themselves—"Poor me"—or it becomes an excuse for everything and not moving on. Ask yourself, "What benefits do I get from holding on to this?" Be honest with yourself. You have a conscious and subconscious knowing; your subconscious always wants you to know, but maybe your conscious is not ready to know. Being honest helps you to know where the lack of knowing is and gives you the chance to work on the blocking issues. The process is like a jigsaw puzzle: you need to put some pieces in place before you are ready for the next step or knowing. Validating your feelings is primary. "I do not want to forgive yet" may open the way to forgive. Examining the benefits of holding onto the hurt can help you see how the hurt plays itself out in other situations and relationships in your life. The benefits of forgiveness usually outweigh the holding on to hurt. Say to yourself, "I am ready to give up and let go of the wounds," and take back what you were robbed of.

Forgiveness is not outside as much as inside. The lack of forgiveness produces stress. Stress can cause physical, mental, and spiritual disorders. This is another good reason for progressing to forgiveness. Negativity is another excuse used for the failure to grow. "Well, that is just the way I am" is the excuse used. But it is really possible to change that too. Is the glass half-full or half-empty? It is a choice, and it may be the hardest to change, but change it can. You first have to believe you can change. We live in a negative culture; remember, take something in small doses, as the negativity can suck the energy right out of you and make you feel hopeless and helpless. Read the Sunday paper only; as it has all the weekly news. Watch the six o'clock news and not the eleven o'clock, as going to bed on negativity is not good for you. It is the first thing you process in your sleep. Make sure you go to bed on a positive note or pleasant circumstances. Forgiveness, for instance, is positive.

Everything is energy. Thinking is energy. Negativity is energy. It will drain you of positive energy. That is why we need to take negativity in small doses. You can teach old dogs new tricks, so no matter how long you have been negative, you can learn to be more positive. First, be willing to change, then be realistic and try only one idea at a time, or you will become overwhelmed. Now, call an A's an A's, be factual, but that is different than seeing everything positive or negative. If someone says, "It is a beautiful day," and it is snowing out, if you see it as negative, you are failing to see the beauty in the fresh falling snow. Stop the next time and be able to see the beauty. If someone says, "I hate snow," be able to find a positive activity using the snow, like skiing, sledding, or building a fire in the fireplace. Seeing the negative is draining and stressful. It saps our energy. It makes better sense to reserve our energy for uplifting, positive functions that give more joy and enhance life around us.

Some people just do not want to be happy, or they feel they do not deserve to be happy. It is a way of life for some. This is a good point to ponder and process about yourself; it may be what stops your potential from coming to the surface. You just do not feel good enough. Culturally, that message is out there everywhere, but it was and likely will always be out there for those who want an excuse for why things cannot be different. You cannot change others, but you can change what is inside you. You can believe that you deserve and are good enough, you have enough, and you are enough. Shut out the interference from outside, and get to what is in you. If you want to let go of negativity, you will; if you do not, then you will not. No more excuses—it is really up to you. We only change self, but we can influence change in others, and the best way is to stop feeding their negativity.

Eastern cultures pursue longevity, not from the fear of ageing, which is inconsistent with reincarnation, but because they desire to maximize the time available to perfect themselves in this life and therefore allow themselves the opportunity to live their lives free from the burden of the unwanted baggage that they call karma. Western culture has a saying, "What goes around comes around," which can be called karma. "What you sow, you will reap" is also karma. This really says there is nothing new under the sun. There really is not, for it is all there for the discovery. When we discover the self, we discover everything else. "Been there, done that" says that we will all go there if we have not already. We are all somewhere on the path, each on her/his own journey, some starting where others have just been, and how far or fast you go in this lifetime really does not matter; it is all up to you.

Again, the US culture is adolescent, so it cannot help you go beyond adolescence. If you want to mature beyond that, then you will have to go inside yourself. This is not good or bad, as you, having no choice but to go inside, will find a wealth of insights there. The contradictions will become more clearly defined for you. Remember, you are being told by our government that you do not know what is good for you, so you need laws, and the statement used is that they are looking out for your best interest, when they are looking out for their best interests. The good here is that with all the contradictions, you have the frustration to motivate you to review what is being said and done in the name of your best interest. If there were not a thorn in your side, you and the rest of us would go on our merry way, but the thorns in our sides force us to pay attention. If it did not hurt, you would not pay attention. No pain, no gain. The pain is positive, as we need it to pierce our skin to help us grow. When you are ready to say, "You made me do it," stop and remember that no one makes you do anything—you choose to. If individuals think, feel, and do, then our government does too. Our government is just a group of individuals. However, it is easier to influence others if the group agrees and says, "It is in your best interest that we do this or that." Once you know who you are or what you want to be, you will not be so easily led astray. You will be okay at being the self and not be a sheep to slaughter.

Issues around not being part of the group are abandonment and rejection. If you are fearful of either abandonment or rejection because of your past experiences, than your first step is to deal with these two issues in order for the self to be okay at not following the sheep. Remember, your fears are there to help you overcome fears, not avoid them. Abandonment and rejection are not in your life just to irritate you, but to help you grow. Work on them until you no longer feel their sting. Most of our culture, at one time or another, has had to process these issues. No one really escapes the fears totally. Again, look at them as positive, as opportunities to grow and learn. Become survivors of them and no longer victims. Do not let them run your life anymore. Both abandonment and rejection can help you on your path, as they give you a focus, different than if they were never in your life. I like to think these experiences and more build our character. Try not to be "poor me" in all of this, as it is one sure way to stunt growth. The purpose of life is to become all you can become, and along the way there are many issues that can help or hinder your growth. So much energy can be spent in our lives by wishing some things never happened. They did, so come to terms with them, so learning and growing can be the results of their happening. Everything happens for a reason, it really does. "What is this trying to teach me?" is a good place to start when confronted with an issue that needs to be processed or resolved.

DEATH AND DYING

Culturally, our biggest fears are around death and dying. Most state that it is not dying that is the biggest fear, but how they will die. Fear of where they are going is very primary. Since most believe in a heaven and hell, then it is where they are going that gives them great concerns. Death is not possible according to most religions. That is, you have eternal life. The meaning of eternal life is, however, different for many persons, as it should be. But for many it is very confusing.

We certainly understand that this body does not live forever, so it must be the spirit or soul that lives forever. It helps if you go to the belief that we are made in the image of God. It cannot be physical, therefore it is spiritual. Spirit is energy. So the eternal part of you is spirit or energy. The mind is also energy, and it goes with your spirit when you die. Our fears have come mainly from the lack of good teachings by our churches. It is important that you understand this, so in the future, you will not fear questioning ideas when they do not ring true. Never give up your own power and control. I-lose that we believe to be experts are not always experts; they are in the process of becoming also. It was conditional love that was taught in mainline churches in our Lois B. Mayette culture, and that gave the churches too much power and control over your view of where you were going when you died. Now this brings us back to God being unconditional love. Again, there is no hell, lest you believe there is or you create one. Trust yourself and God that there is not one, as God is unconditional love. In the past teaching, it certainly seemed like he was a conditional God. That may be difficult for you to process, as you may want the bad guys to get their just reward.

Now here is the kicker in that: you then have to use the same yardstick on yourself as you want used on others. That will likely put you back to square one, where you are not worthy of God's love. God does not make junk, and he declares that everyone is worthy. God is unconditional love. Adolescence wants everyone to get theirs, but maturity does not. Since our culture is adolescence, most in our culture have not likely experienced unconditional love but conditional love.

Marriage and parenting are the two most difficult relationships in the universe, but are also where the most growing can take place. Most of marriage and parenting in our culture is based on conditional love. "What is in it for me?" Parents identify too much with the success or failure of their children. The bumper sticker that says "My child is an honor student" can be honoring the child, or it could be saying, "See, I've done a good job, and it is bragging rights." If you have ever said to your child, or remember your parents saying, "But you could have done better," then that was conditional love.

Marriage in our culture is very conditional. "What's in it for me? rather than "Together we will help each other become all we can become." Expecting someone else to be in charge of your happiness will never work, as you are in charge of your own happiness. It is never up to someone else what we become. The devil cannot make you do it! You are in charge of the self. %ere is a possessiveness in our marriages. No one owns anyone else. Talk about a turn-off! No one wants to be possessed. It is really "free to be me" that everyone is moving towards. Unconditional love is letting others, as well as self, learn at their own pace, in their own time, and in their own way. We see right and wrong, and there is none. God certainly let us have free will, so let others have free will; is it not your goal to be God-like?

If birth is positive, then death is positive. Death certainly leaves a void for those left behind, but for the dead, there is the joy of returning home. Remember, we are spiritual beings having a human experience. So home it is, back to spirit again. If you know this, then death will be less fearful; the spirit will know where to go and what is expected. If you have a traumatic death, you could have some confusion at death; spiritually. But if you know the process more, then it will be less confusing.

Now, the big advantage of processing your beliefs on death and dying is that it frees you up to live. The greatest fear no longer being a fear helps process all other fears. It makes the process easier, as the lesser fears will have fewer unknowns to the process. Let us take the fear of failure. It is likely number nine on the scale of one to ten, ten being fear of death and dying. Fear of failure is big in our culture. The process with fear of failure is first, how you view your control in it. Are you fearing your disappointment or the disappointment of others? If others, then work on the view others have of you. You have no control over their view of you, so let go of that. Now look at your view of yourself. Why do you feel anything is a failure? Why isn't it worth the experience in growth and development? So, "Try, try again" would be a good motto. It is not a failure; it is a learning, growing experience. Lighten up and try again. Who says you have to succeed the first time? Love the challenge and experience as in a win-win experience.

Death of a loved one requires the five steps of grieving: denial, bargaining, anger, depression, and acceptance. When death occurs to a loved one, family or friend, we usually go through the five steps to grieve. The first is denial. This stage is not very long as a general rule. If there is a body, then reality will set in faster. If there is no body for a long time or ever, that closure and realness will cake longer. Did you ever get a call that someone has died and ask the caller if they were sure? Well, do not be surprised, as others have done that also. It is part of the denial. The next steps can go together or one by one, and not necessarily in a specific order. Bargaining, depression, and anger may all happen together and at the same time. Bargaining may also be very brief, like just asking for more time, making a statement of wishing it did not happen, or a desire to trade places: "Why not me? I have had a good long life. It was too soon or sudden. I wish I had done this or that." Unfinished business is part of the bargaining. The more we view that the death should not have taken place, the more wishful thinking will take place.

Depression can be spread all over the void. Do not expect it to go away anytime soon; that would be a mistake. Tie greater the loss, the longer the depression. We say one to seven years for the loss of a significant other. You never forget the person; the pain just gets more bearable as time goes on. Depression will go away in time if you process and do not just stuff it down. We miss the person forever, but depression should not be there forever. Your views on death and dying may need some rethinking at this time.

Anger is important. You might say, "Who or what do I get angry at?" First, the deceased loved one—yes, the deceased. You would not feel as you do if they had not died. You might think, well, it was not their fault. And it isn't about fault—it is about the void. So, get angry. This too may be very short-lived. You can also be angry at others who are still alive. Process the anger and realize it is okay to have these extreme feelings. Let them be your teacher to a better understanding of death and dying.

Acceptance is the final step but may be there before the process is very far along: the acceptance that is finally needed is that life goes on, but differently, and missing them maybe forever, but memories are forever. Think on good times and the learning or joy they gave your life.

Give yourself permission to cry for as long as you like or it takes. Be real with the process; do not try to get over it, as others may want you to. Everyone is different; do not use comparisons. You likely will not know where, when, or how something will hit you in the grieving for some time. Crying anywhere is a good growing experience. The more you have invested in a relationship, the bigger the loss and void and the longer the pain, likely.

THERE ARE MORE UNKNOWNS THAN KNOWNS

Remember the elusive energy, the more than five senses, and what we call sometimes the supernatural? As you grow in wisdom, it becomes more apparent that there are more unknowns than knowns. Wisdom is defined as gaining knowledge, insight, or wisdom about a course of action. It is important that one is willing to realize that we know very little, rather than the idea that we know much, as then you will want to unlock the mysteries of life. is one of the key elements needed to finding the knowledge of the unknowns or mysteries of the universe and beyond.

Science fiction has been an interest to many, and Harry Potter has given back to some the spark to unlock the mind to search for other realms. For so long, it was not in vogue to question what was said to be already known. Our education and churches were two institutions that squashed exploring "what ifs." Both institutions are in great need of revising. Both teach much that was never the truth, so therefore should let go of the untruths and leave more time for things that matter and are useful. Our children in schools are being asked to test well to prove that the state or the teachers are doing a good job. Much of the time, it has little to do with the wellbeing of the child or what individual children are all about. Children are sheep to slaughter for the convenience of others. In New York State, 56% more students are labeled with some kind of disability in learning 1983. Mind you, this may be on either end of the spectrum, too bright or not bright enough. Something is wrong with this picture. BOCES cost the state of New York more than the regular school system. Healthy

New York? I think not. Boys are labeled twice as much as females. Functioning of the brain differences are the reason given for this. It is more likely the development of the brain that accounts for difference. Since males show less emotions and have fewer outlets for their energy, the brain is not developing as the female brain does. This is why it is important for the male to get in touch with his female side or develop the verbal skills and emotions more. Role models are very important at an early age. Fostering this development is not difficult; both parents need to be on the same page. They need to decide that together, they will help each sex to have the full range of emotions. If parents decide that they do not want either sex to relate too strongly as feminine or masculine, then likely the children will not relate too strongly to one sex or the other. They will have a healthier range of emotions.

Most churches, as said before, teach as if God died some 2006 years ago and he is not teaching new ideas today. Well that certainly helps with the decline of the churches in attendance. The church is a good foundation, but can be boring after that. How many times do you want the same scripture read and explained the same way each time?

God speaks to people today as much as he ever has. What is he saying? God has to be bored with us, as we are certainly stuck and afraid. We are afraid of the new and unknown. book *The Da Vinci Code* was a breath of fresh air for many, as we love the mystery and are starving for new ideas and where God is today.

Intuition is defined as the power of knowing things without conscious reasoning, or quick and ready insight. It is one of those senses that is beyond the five senses that we are very familiar with. Intuition has a lot to do with self-esteem, in that a good self-esteem will foster trust and faith in yourself, lending to a questioning mind, so when things just do not ring true, you will not doubt yourself and will check out further learning. In Germany in 1992, what the three of us talked about while waiting for Gorbachev was why the US citizens seemed to lack the ability to question direction and issues, to be more well-rounded. Thinking did not seem to be in vogue. Intuition is squashed at an early age, sometimes because parents are so unaware and afraid of questions they do not know how to answer. Parents fear their children not fitting the status quo, the status quo being better than average. Everyone should read, Dr. Burns' book *Feeling Good*, especially the chapter "Dare to be Average." Perfectionists are likely not to get to the top, as they live in a lot of fear: fear of failure, fear of being wrong, fear of being different, or fear of conflicts. Perfectionists spin their gears, going nowhere, because they are to busy checking and rechecking their endeavors. This is very familiar to me, as I am a perfectionist. I like to think it is in remission, but not before I gave it to three children. Parents say that they do not want to push their children but are afraid it will hurt the child if they work at a different pace than the school's. Home schooling is greatly on the rise, but much of that is for the wrong reasons. The right reasons should be to cut out some of the unnecessary learning, being able to teach the facts better, or teaching the same material in a lot less time and making it fun to learn. I went to a one-room schoolhouse for five years, from the third grade to the eighth. Best experience of my life. Science was nature and, in the woods, math was hands-on, and reading was fun, as we had prose and poetry. This was the best mind training, as we had long recitals and plays. Many children could skip the eighth grade, as, after hearing everything for a few years, you knew the eighth grade before you got there. I did not test out the first time taking the eighth-grade regents, not because I did not know the material, but because my fears and anxiety got in the way of my retrieving the information that I knew well. The big school, crowds, and fears left me out of my comfort zone. It was also a good lesson, as I was not ready for the big school and did well the next years. Things happen for a reason, and not a negative reason. What comes to mind now are some of the experiments on animals and how, once trained, the animals refuse for some time to recognize the change in the experiment. People are no different; they saw it work yesterday, so it must work today, and when it does not, they just push harder to make the old work. Let's understand that what worked yesterday was for yesterday, and today is calling for change. Culturally, we fear change, yet the only thing constant is change. Why do bad things happen? Because they need to. What you need in your life will be there to help you grow and learn. Did you ever work through a problem and then find it disappear, when it had been in your face for so long? Where did it go? How about the person in your face all the time, and when you came to terms with them, their behavior and your feelings were no longer in conflict? Why was that? Do you ever learn about something new and then find it everywhere you look? Was it there all the time and you just did not have a frame of reference for it? Yes, it was there, but you were oblivious to its existence.

You needed the experience, so we need to understand that it is in your face for a good reason. Now deal with it by learning how to see it in a different light. Things irritate us until we see them in a more realistic light. Let us take the boss in your face that is just unreasonable. Call an A's an A's. It is not that you are not experiencing it just like it is—it is that you need to ask why it is this way and what you can learn from it. Willingness to learn makes all the difference in the world. Note, I did not say "He is doing it to you," as he is not. You have choices. The boss is your teacher. It is the way you look at what is happening that counts. Become more positive and realistic to change our feelings of anger and irritation. Just because his/her title is boss does not mean he/she has finished his/her journey. See how you might welcome something from them, then see how you might see their task and pressure differently. Thinking is the powerhouse. You will be surprised at how fast he/she changes. (My joke.) He/she does not change—it is your view that changed, therefore your feelings and behavior change too. Many have said that is just a mind game. No, it is more positive and realistic. Strive to be realistic. A perfectionist is not wrong; a perfectionist is just unrealistic, usually about a fair, just, and perfect world. If it was a fair, just world, then your ideals would work—but it is a fair, just world. Being rigid and inflexible are real issues for the perfectionist. Being comfortable in your own skin and having a good sense of self will help you navigate through issues and problems in your world.

Trust and faith in yourself will help you with intuition, so you will have less doubt about what that still, small voice is trying to convey to you. Intuition is the spirit within or without, trying to get you to move in or understand beyond your norm. It is very important to growth and development. The more you trust in intuition, the more you recognize it, and it will increase because you are giving it attention and believing in it. There is no luck or coincidences; everything happens for a reason. Practicing intuition, or the still, small voice, will also increase your awareness. The awareness of how everything fits together for the moving ahead or evolving in your personal life and in the life of the universe. There will be less worry about what is happening and the outcome in situations, but concern will be there. Concern needs to be there or change would not take place.

It looks like things are hidden from us more than they are. Life is a process. We get caught up in first, the survival phase; next, the learning phase; then the awareness phase; and then, hopefully, the teaching phase. There can be other phases; one could be called the relearning phase and another called the letting-go phase. In Hinduism, mankind's life is to be divided into four phases: first, being born, then as a student and serving others. Second, householder or role in the world (materialistic).

Third, retirement to the forest to meditate (spiritual growth). Fourth, as a wondering sage or teacher, giving away what you know. The last phase is *moksa*, which is a technique of transcending the senses in order to discover, know, and dwell at one with the timeless reality which underlies the dream of life in the world, the metaphysical.

Most humans move like the walking dead, this phase being the survival phase. They are not aware of why they move and who or what the master mind is, the mind behind that which moves them. The walking dead are oblivious to their creator or their fellow human beings. Mind being energy and metaphysical. Most humans are seekers of God rather than believers. Seekers are not good or bad, but rather they are going through a phase very necessary for growth and understanding. The churches and religious reading are important in this phase, whether you are Christian, Moslem, Buddhist, or Hindu. It is the foundation needed to move forward to the next phase. The spiritual journey, if taking a holistic approach to life, will filter throughout all phases of life. Those who do not have the holistic approach always feel like something is missing in their lives, and there is, since we are spiritual beings having a human experience. You need to be feeding your spiritual needs. Spirituality is the center of most cultures. The US started out being a colony for religious freedom, which it seems at times we have walked away from, as we are too much into the world as flesh. Why is a fall needed? So we can get back to basics, which is important.

In the survival phase, there is a great deal of dependence on others and your environment. baby is very dependent. Your born-again experience is a very dependent phase. It is very important that you do not get stuck there, as it is just the foundation, the awakening. The learning phase is less dependent, and more time is there for questioning. The love of learning is exciting, to the point that you may not be aware of anything beyond the learning. Jesus got upset when the people kept wanting more miracles. Some people are quick to learn, and some never seem to learn; everyone else is somewhere in between. Jesus had a good reason to be upset, as miracles were to be encouragers for furthering your faith. If he kept doing miracles, it would stop you from learning. Each step you learn is a prerequisite for the next step. Imagination is important in challenging your old beliefs. It takes the baby steps to move ahead to the giant steps. So a miracle could be seen as omitting the baby steps and the learning necessary for the next learning. If you do not learn to multiply, then division will not make sense, and it will make division harder. United States is adolescence at its best. We are stuck there. Miracles are not always positive in first light, or what we think of as positive. They all turn out to be positive in the end, as growing takes place, and that is always positive. So if disaster hits the universe, it is there to help us grow. It turns out to further life and be positive.

The next phase after learning is the awareness phase. This phase takes the learning to another level of usefulness in exploring the unknown, as at this level you realize you know very little. What lies beyond is questioning that which does not make sense. Learning uncovers the contradiction and dichotomies. In the past, the churches asked us not to go there, perhaps because they did not know, and asked us to accept it in faith. Dichotomies are not always going to reveal the answers, but do not think it has anything to do with faith. It has to do with our limited abilities. lack of knowing forces us to question what we do not know or think we do not know, for in reality we or spirit knows everything already. So we are basically uncovering what is already known, or we are remembering. Mankind is able to obtain truth by the intense search into the deepest recesses of all categories of the natural or supernatural phenomena, as stated before. You have the ability, but there is a lot of hard work ahead. Hard work may be the wrong idea here, as it is really letting go that is needed: letting go of the ego that thinks it has arrived but is really stuck. It is important to challenge old assumptions and beliefs. Awareness is just that: being aware beyond the physical to the metaphysical. "Metaphysical" is defined as the mind in the universe. Hard work maybe a misnomer, but you cannot be lazy and find out what the mind of the universe wants for you. You cannot get it from others, as you are unique. If you believe as everyone else, you are not unique or will you find your uniqueness. To the universe, you are important, a unique, important individual. You now have to go inside, to the unique or special you.

Now, once you have the necessary awareness, the next phase is teacher or sage, giving away the understanding as you see it. Not as in pushing or shoving it down someone else's throat, but teaching others, not caring who, what, where, or when. No real need for an outcome— just pass it on. Confucius said, 'Those who are meant to hear will understand. Those who are not meant to understand will not hear.

ABOUT THE AUTHOR

Lois B. Mayette, is a seasoned psychotherapist in private practice, as a certified licensed social worker in New York State. She is a graduate of SUNT at Sony Brook with a masters in social work.

She has always taken a holistic approach to wholeness; body, mind and spirit. This book is complied from her journals and writings, collected over some 35 plus years.

She is a parent, grandparent and lives in Watertown, New York, where she still practices as psychotherapist.